MAINTAIN
OR
TRANSFORM

MAINTAIN OR TRANSFORM

How to Lead with Standards, Build Strong Teams, and Execute Through Change

CARLOS E. GUTIERREZ FERRETE

Paperback ISBN: 979-8-9952094-0-9
Hardcover ISBN: 979-8-9952094-1-6
eBook ISBN: 979-8-9952094-2-3

First Edition

Published by
GUFER Leadership Press
United States of America

DEDICATION

To My Family

To my family—thank you for your love, your patience, and your steady belief in me, especially during seasons when the outcome was unclear and the path was still forming.

Leadership is often visible in results, but rarely in the sacrifices that precede them. You lived those sacrifices with me. You endured transitions, uncertainty, relocations, long hours, and moments where the vision required faith before it produced evidence. Your support was not passive—it was an active partnership.

This journey was never mine alone. Every decision to grow, to move, to transform, affected you first. Your resilience strengthened mine. Your trust reinforced my conviction. If this book reflects discipline, ownership, and perseverance, it is because those values were sustained at home long before they were expressed at work.

This is as much your story as it is mine.

To the Leaders Who Shaped Me — and the Teams Who Trusted Me

To the leaders who raised my standards and challenged my assumptions—thank you for modeling what accountability, excellence, and courage look like in practice. You showed me that leadership is not about authority; it is about responsibility.

Some of you pushed me harder than I thought necessary at the time. In hindsight, those moments refined my discipline. You did not lower expectations to make things easier. You raised them to make me better.

To the teams and organizations who trusted me to lead—you gave me the opportunity to test these principles in real environments, with real consequences. Leadership is not a theory. It is practiced in complex, high-pressure, and uncertain environments. Thank you for the trust, the candor, and the partnership that allowed growth to occur on both sides of the table.

Any framework in these pages has been shaped by real people, real operations, and real stakes.

To My Father

To my father, who passed before holding this book, but whose influence is woven into every page.

You always shared your leadership journey with me—the roles you held, the responsibilities you carried, the defining moments of your career, and, most importantly, how to become successful. But success, as you taught it, was never about titles or recognition. It was about becoming excellent at what you do and helping others rise along the way.

You believed everything should be done with excellence. There were no small responsibilities. There were only opportunities to demonstrate character.

Your mantra was simple: aim to be the best in what you do. Work where you feel passion, and it will never feel like a job.

This book carries your imprint.

This is part of your legacy, too.

ACKNOWLEDGEMENTS

Leadership is never built alone.

To the teams I had the privilege to lead: thank you.

You carried standards when pressure rose. You adapted when change required discipline. You chose ownership when it would have been easier to protect comfort. You showed that performance is not just about hitting numbers—it is about consistency, accountability, and pride in the work.

Through transitions, growth, setbacks, and transformation, you reinforced a simple truth: culture is not declared; it is practiced daily. The progress we achieved together was never the result of a single decision or a single leader, but of shared commitment and mutual trust.

Leadership may carry one name at the top—but momentum, resilience, and excellence are always collective.

This book reflects experiences we built together.

CONTENTS

INTRODUCTION

There was a point early in my career when the path ahead of me was clear, stable, and respectable. I had invested years in my education. I had earned credentials that provided security. I had momentum. By most standards, I was on track. And I chose to disrupt it.

The decision to leave that stability and start over in the United States was not a reckless leap. It was shaped first by responsibility. I had come to understand that the environment in which you build your life matters as much as the goals you pursue within it. Stability without safety is fragile. Predictability without long-term opportunity is limiting. If I were going to build a future for myself and my family, it needed to rest on a stronger foundation.

At the same time, relocation offered broader professional possibilities. The move was not purely about career advancement, but it was not disconnected from it either. If we were going to start over, it would be with intention. The decision carried trade-offs: leaving familiarity, rebuilding credibility, navigating immigration constraints, and competing in a different market without the advantage of history or network. Stability was available. Growth was uncertain.

Starting over required more than ambition. It required resilience. Early in my roles in the United States, I operated daily in a second language—presenting, influencing, and leading in environments where communication precision matters. I often prepared twice as long as others. I rehearsed conversations. I rewrote emails. I translated ideas in my head before expressing them out loud. The standards

I set for myself did not adjust simply because the context became more difficult.

There were moments when progress slowed. Moments when credentials did not immediately translate into opportunity. Moments when maintaining what was secure would have been easier to justify.

Looking back, I recognize that this period introduced a decision pattern that would define my leadership journey: Maintain what is comfortable. Or transform toward what is possible.

That tension does not disappear as responsibility increases. It evolves. Early in a career, it may show up in personal risk—whether to relocate, to pursue additional education, to leave a stable role that limits growth. As leadership scope expands, the same decision reappears in different forms: whether to raise hiring standards, whether to confront cultural complacency, whether to invest in transformation before external pressure demands it, and whether to address underperformance when tolerance feels easier than confrontation.

Individuals drift toward maintaining. Organizations do the same. Systems are designed to preserve what exists. Processes protect stability. Comfort becomes normalized. The role of leadership is not to eliminate stability—it is to ensure that stability does not quietly become stagnation.

The discipline to transform requires structured thinking under uncertainty. It requires the willingness to accept short-term discomfort in the service of long-term capability. It requires ownership—the refusal to wait for ideal conditions before acting. Over time, this lens shaped how I evaluate opportunity, build teams, enforce standards, design operating rhythms, and approach change.

This book is not a memoir. It is a decision lens. It is for leaders early in their journey who sense that comfort may be limiting growth. It is for leaders who feel stuck in a cycle and are looking for a disciplined way forward. It is for those with long-term aspirations who need structure to translate vision into action. And it is for leaders operating at scale who understand that the same choice—maintain or transform—determines whether organizations merely survive or deliberately build enduring capability.

Leadership is not built in comfort. It is built in decisions. And the decisions we make—especially when stability is available—compound over time. They shape our trajectory, our teams, and ultimately the legacy we leave behind.

Part I — The Foundation

CHAPTER 1: Career-Defining Moments

We all have experiences that change us, often without labels. In the moment, they feel like uncertainty, discomfort, or disruption. Only later do we recognize them as career-defining moments—experiences that force us to choose who we want to become.

My leadership journey didn't start with confidence; it began with vulnerability, uncertainty, and choices that required me to move forward before I felt ready.

1995–1996: Vulnerability and the First Definition of Success

In October 1995, just as I was approaching my graduation, I found myself in a situation that would forever alter my perspective on life and leadership. I was kidnapped in Mexico City, an event that thrust me into a world of fear and uncertainty.

It happened one night as I was returning home from a party. A car suddenly crossed my path, and four men stepped out, forcing me into their vehicle. They tossed me into the back seat, covering my head with a plastic bag, and positioned two of them on either side of me. I could feel a gun pressed against one of my kidneys, a chilling reminder of my helplessness. They took all my possessions—my jewelry, wallet, and money—before driving to a couple of ATMs to withdraw cash until they reached my withdrawal limit.

My heart raced as we stopped in front of my subdivision, where the security guard, who recognized me, called out my name and asked if everything was okay. The kidnappers must have realized that people would start looking for me immediately, as they decided not to take me for a longer ride. Instead, they left me on a dark street. As I got out of the car, they warned me to walk away and threatened to shoot me if I turned around.

With adrenaline coursing through me, I began walking, but as soon as I heard the sound of their car driving away, I sprinted in the opposite direction until I reached a busier street. I finally calmed down and, feeling a mix of relief and disbelief, I hailed a cab and went home, shaken but alive.

Surviving that ordeal left me not just physically unharmed but profoundly changed. Upon my release, I became acutely aware of the vulnerability that exists in positions of power—how easily it can be abused—and I learned to respect authority without ever taking it for granted. This experience ignited a sense of intentionality within me, steering my career toward leadership that emphasized empathy, clarity, and accountability.

Graduating in 1996 filled me with pride—not because it was easy, but because it wasn't. I felt exhausted and excited to finally start my career.

First Job: Learning Organizational Dynamics

My first formal job was as a Project Engineer at Frito-Lay's Continuous Improvement department. I joined a rotational program for recent graduates that exposed us to various parts of the organization.

My first leader, Edmundo Arechiga, significantly impacted my understanding of leadership. We were similar—curious and direct. Through him, I learned how organizations make decisions: sometimes with data, sometimes without, and sometimes too late due to over-analysis. I also learned that good leaders listen; ignoring employees' perspectives has consequences.

Years later, I would replicate a similar rotational program for five years. At the time, I didn't realize it was the first brick in my leadership foundation.

1999: A Second Wake-Up Call

By 1999, I was on my third job, enjoying momentum but lacking direction. That year, I experienced another attempted kidnapping. The clarity was immediate: I didn't want to raise a family in Mexico under those conditions. Staying meant accepting a risk I couldn't pass on to my family.

So, I laid out a plan—not a dream—a plan for graduate school in supply chain management. I quit my job, sold my car, and committed fully, knowing there were no guarantees. Leaving meant sacrificing daily access to family and friends and raising children without a support system. That was the cost. But the alternative felt worse.

2000–2002: Starting Over

In June 2000 at 27, I moved to Madison, Wisconsin, to attend ESL school, surrounded by 18-year-olds. I treated ESL like a job—school all day, homework at night, never embarrassed to ask questions.

Graduate school at MIT was even harder. Academically demanding and intense, I felt technically confident but insecure verbally. Then came 9/11; the job market froze. I faced over twenty rejections and the risk of losing my student housing.

Eventually, I landed my first job in the U.S. at H-E-B in Texas, thanks to Al Barrientez III, the leader who took a chance on me. That decision changed my life, marking the beginning of stability and sponsorship in the U.S.

2005–2007: Progress and Reset

In 2005, while working at H-E-B, I relocated back to Mexico for visa purposes and was promoted to Director of Supply Chain. It was a validating experience after spending years building credibility with my team. However, after 18 months in Mexico, I realized I couldn't stay; with our third child on the way, remaining there meant I would likely never return to the U.S.

In 2007, I returned to the U.S. in a lower role—Senior Manager—in a department that didn't welcome me. Despite having been with the company for 5 years, I felt like a stranger. It wasn't ego that bothered me; it was purpose.

So, I asked to move into warehousing, leading the export and the seasonal warehouses; two years later, I was leading one of the largest facilities in the network. Titles didn't matter; capability did.

2013–2014: Leading With Autonomy

In 2013, I left H-E-B after ten years to join C&S Wholesale Grocers. I moved to a small town to lead a distribution center with nearly 500 employees—one of the most challenging operations in the network. We lived in a hotel for three months with four kids, facing isolation and winter.

The role taught me how to lead with minimal support and a lot of autonomy. My leader, Hal Leddy, gave me space to operate. I focused on fairness, consistency, and clarity. Trust followed.

Fourteen months later, after changing the culture and improving key metrics, I was promoted and relocated to Florida to run a region.

2016–2021: Applying the Pattern at Scale

In 2016, I joined Reyes Beverage Group as a General Manager and was promoted to Senior Vice President of Operations in 2017. By 2021, I became Chief Supply Chain Officer. Leaders like Frank Schwipe, Ray Guerin, and Tom Day played crucial roles—not by micromanaging but by trusting me to lead.

A clear pattern emerged:

- Lead from the driver's seat
- Focus on what matters
- Raise the talent bar
- Choose growth over comfort

The Thread That Connects It All

Looking back at 1995, what would surprise me most isn't the titles, but that the goal to build a life in the U.S. became a platform for developing others. Success evolved to mean delivering results while creating paths for young leaders.

Leadership is not a race; it's a journey shaped by experiences, not timelines. At every critical moment, I faced the same choice: maintain or transform? This book is about those choices and the lessons they teach.

Leadership Is Built Through Career-Defining Moments

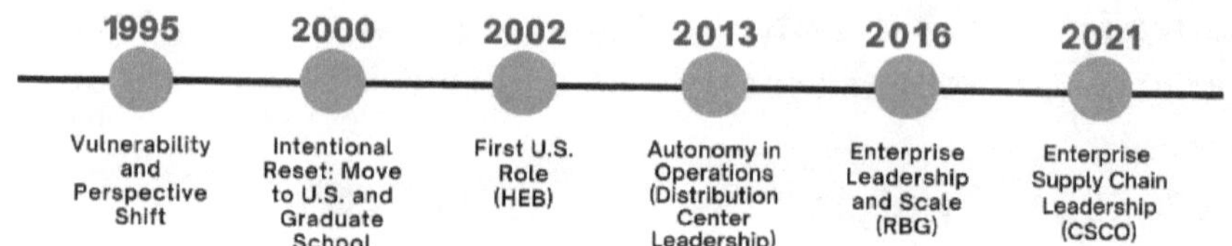

Leadership is not a race; it's a journey shaped by experiences, not timelines.

Career-defining moments rarely feel significant in real time—but they shape the leader you become.

Key Takeaways

- Career-defining moments often stem from experiences that push you out of your comfort zone.

- Leadership is defined by decisions made during challenging times, not by titles.

- Vulnerability and discomfort can reveal transformative opportunities; act on them.

- Both positive or negative experiences shape our leadership journey and enhance decision-making.

Reflection Question

What career-defining moments have shaped your leadership journey, and how have they influenced your decisions?

CHAPTER 2: Maintain or Transform

Every career reaches moments where progress slows—not because effort disappears, but because momentum does. These moments don't always feel dramatic. Often, they show up quietly: a role that feels familiar, a job you can do well without stretching, a routine that works. On the surface, everything looks fine.

That's when the real decision appears:

Do you maintain—or do you transform?

This question has followed me throughout my career, long before I had language for it. I didn't invent it as a framework. I lived it first— repeatedly—across roles, countries, and leadership stages.

Looking back, the biggest inflection points in my journey were not promotions or titles. They were decisions about whether to protect what was comfortable or pursue what would force growth.

The Difference Between Maintaining and Transforming

Maintaining is not a failure. Maintainers preserve stability. They protect systems that work. They ensure continuity, reliability, and predictability. Organizations need maintainers. Teams rely on them.

Not every moment calls for disruption. But maintaining becomes a problem when it turns into avoidance.

Transformation, on the other hand, requires intention. It demands that you question what exists and ask whether it still serves the future you are trying to build. Transformation introduces discomfort, risk, and uncertainty—but it also creates momentum.

The mistake many leaders make is thinking this is a personality trait. It's not. It's a choice—one that shows up repeatedly over time.

The Maintain or Transform Decision Model

<table>
<tr><td>MAINTAIN</td><td>THE FILTER:
Am I protecting comfort or building future capability?</td><td>TRANSFORM</td></tr>
<tr><td>

- Protects Comfort
- Preserves Stability
- Limited or Incremental Growth
- Question: Am I staying because it is safe?

</td><td></td><td>

- Builds Capability
- Creates Momentum
- Accelerated Growth
- Expands Leadership Range
- Question: Am I willing to embrace uncertainty?

</td></tr>
</table>

Maintaining is not failure, but comfort becomes stagnation when it turns into avoidance.

Every meaningful leadership inflection point begins with this decision: protect comfort—or expand capability. The strongest leaders choose capability, even when the outcome is uncertain.

Why This Decision Matters More Than You Think

Early in my career, I believed hard work alone would create opportunity. And hard work does matter. But effort without intentional change often leads to stagnation. I've seen people work incredibly hard while staying exactly where they are.

Transformation doesn't require abandoning everything at once. In fact, sustainable transformation rarely looks dramatic in the moment.

It often starts with small but deliberate shifts:

- Taking a role that stretches you laterally
- Asking to learn a part of the business you don't understand
- Moving toward complexity instead of away from it
- Choosing a harder assignment when an easier one is available

Each of these decisions carries uncertainty. None of them guarantees immediate reward. But over time, they compound.

The Cost of Maintaining (When It Becomes Comfort)

Maintaining feels safe in the short term. You protect stability. You avoid unnecessary mistakes. You stay inside what you already know. You deliver results in a familiar environment. But here's what people underestimate: Maintaining has a cost too.

Over time, the cost often looks like this:

- Your learning slows down
- Your confidence becomes tied to familiarity
- Your career becomes predictable—but not expanding
- You stop earning new credibility
- You become valuable in one role, but limited beyond it

This is how leaders become stuck—not because they are failing, but because they are comfortable.

Comfort is rarely dangerous on Day 1. It becomes expensive in Year 3.

The Cost of Transforming (And Why It's Worth It)

Transformation is not free either.

It costs you:

- Comfort
- Certainty
- Routine
- Control
- Sometimes even ego

Transformation often looks like stepping into roles where failure is possible.

But transformation gives you something maintaining can't:

Range.

Range builds judgment. Judgment builds credibility. And credibility creates opportunity. Transformation doesn't just make you better at your current job. It prepares you for the next one.

Two Micro-Examples (What This Looks Like in Real Life)

Micro-example #1: Maintaining feels fine—until you realize you're drifting

There are roles where you can perform well without stretching. You know the operation. You know the people. You know the playbook.

And if you're not careful, you start repeating the same year over and over again—just with different numbers.

At first, it feels like stability.

But eventually, you feel it:

You're not growing at the speed you could.

You're not building new capability.

You're simply executing what you already know.

That's not a crisis. But it is a warning sign.

Micro-example #2: Transformation is uncomfortable—but it changes everything

Some of my biggest growth came when I stepped into environments where I wasn't fully ready, and I didn't have the same support system. New teams. New culture. New expectations.

The first months were heavy. High pressure. High stakes. But that discomfort forced faster learning, clearer leadership, and stronger discipline. It wasn't comfortable, but it accelerated everything—because it demanded a better version of me. That's transformation.

Transformation Is Not Reckless Change

One of the most important lessons I learned over the years is this:

Nothing is transformed if it cannot be sustained.

Transformation without discipline becomes chaos. Leaders who chase change without building systems leave organizations exhausted and unstable.

Sustainable transformation requires balance:

- Respect for what works
- Willingness to challenge what no longer does
- Discipline to build mechanisms that endure

This applies not only to organizations but to careers. Every major step in my journey—from leaving Mexico to starting over in the U.S. to accepting roles where failure was a real possibility—was grounded in preparation, not impulse.

The goal was never disruption for its own sake.

The goal was growth with purpose.

Recognizing the Moment

Career-defining moments don't announce themselves. They don't come with clear instructions or guarantees. More often, they arrive disguised as frustration, restlessness, or opportunity wrapped in risk.

You may recognize them when:

- You feel capable but underutilized
- You stop learning at the pace you once did
- Comfort replaces curiosity
- Your work no longer challenges how you think

These moments ask a quiet question:

Is this still moving me forward?

Ignoring that question doesn't stop time.

It simply delays growth.

A Pattern, Not a Moment

Transformation is rarely a single decision. It's a pattern.

The leaders who grow over time are not the ones who transform once and then settle. They are the ones who repeatedly choose development over convenience, learning over ego, and responsibility over title.

This pattern builds:

- Range
- Judgment
- Credibility
- Resilience

It also builds something less visible but more powerful:

Confidence earned through experience.

A Quick Diagnostic

When you're unsure what to do next, here are a few questions that bring clarity fast:

Signs you may be maintaining:

- "I'm good at this job, but I'm not learning much anymore."
- "My weeks look the same, and I'm not being challenged."
- "I avoid roles that could expose weaknesses."
- "I'm staying because it's stable—not because it's building me."

Signs it's time to transform:

- "This scares me a little, and that's why it matters."
- "This move will build a skill I don't have yet."
- "This will expand my range—even if the title doesn't."
- "This challenge will force a stronger version of me."

The decision question:

- Am I protecting comfort—or building capability?

Most leaders do not consciously choose to maintain. They drift into it.

Maintenance rarely announces itself as a decision. It disguises itself as responsibility, prudence, patience, or realism. Over time, what began as temporary stability becomes normalized comfort. And comfort, left unexamined, quietly limits potential.

Transformation is often not absent. It is simply unconsidered.

The most important shift is not immediately choosing transformation. It is recognizing that it exists as an option. Once you begin to see the pattern—once you notice how often you default to preserving instead of progressing—you regain agency. You move from reacting to circumstances to designing your trajectory.

The question is not whether transformation is risky. It is whether maintaining without reflection is riskier. When you begin to recognize the choice more frequently, energy follows awareness. And with awareness comes the possibility of building something larger than what comfort alone would have allowed.

Where We Go Next

If Chapter 1 established why these moments matter, this chapter explains how they shape a career. In the next chapter, we'll move from decisions to discipline.

Because transformation without consistency doesn't last. **Chapter 3: Leadership as a Weekly Practice** will explore how leaders turn intention into habit—and why progress is built one week at a time.

Key Takeaways

- Maintaining is not failure—but comfort can quietly become stagnation.

- Transforming requires discomfort, but it builds range and credibility.

- The cost of maintaining is often delayed; the cost of transforming is immediate.

- Sustainable transformation requires discipline, not impulsiveness.

- The best leaders build growth as a pattern, not a one-time event.

Reflection Question

What are you maintaining today that future growth will require you to transform?

CHAPTER 3: Leadership as a Weekly Practice

Leadership rarely breaks in one dramatic moment. It drifts. One delayed conversation because the week is heavy. One shifted priority because something feels urgent. One standard that moves "just this once." And then another week passes.

Most leaders do not lose clarity in crisis. They lose it in routine. I learned this over time. Leadership is not built in high-visibility moments or public wins. It is built — or eroded — in the ordinary weeks no one applauds.

It is built through repetition.

Why Leadership Fails Without Discipline

Many leaders have good intentions. They want to develop people. They want to create alignment. They want to lead the right way. But intention without structure fades quickly.

Without discipline, leadership becomes reactive. The urgent crowds out the important. People default to habits instead of principles. Over time, even capable leaders drift—because nothing anchors their behavior week after week.

That's when leadership becomes inconsistent. And inconsistency weakens trust faster than almost anything else.

The Power of the Week

A week is long enough to make progress—and short enough to correct course. That's why I began thinking about leadership not in quarters or years, but in weeks.

A weekly cadence forces honesty:

- Did I show up prepared?
- Did I make the tough decision—or delay it?
- Did I develop someone, or just manage work?
- Did I reinforce priorities—or allow noise to take over?

Weeks don't lie. You can't hide behind a strong quarter if your weeks are weak. You can't claim culture if your weekly behaviors contradict it.

Leadership lives in what you consistently do when no one is watching—and when no one is applauding.

What a Weekly Practice Actually Looks Like

Leadership as a weekly practice is not about adding more meetings or rituals. It's about intentional repetition. For me, it meant creating space—every week—to step out of execution mode and back into leadership mode. To reflect, recalibrate, and refocus.

That practice evolved over time, but the core questions stayed consistent:

- What matters most right now?
- Where am I avoiding a decision?
- Who needs clarity—not reassurance?
- Who am I developing this week?

These questions are simple. Answering them honestly is not.

A Real Example: The Monday Reset That Prevents Drift

Most leaders don't lose the standard in one big moment. They lose it in small moments—one week at a time. One week, you delay a hard conversation because volume is heavy. One week, you accept weak performance because staffing is short. One week, you allow a priority to shift because someone senior asked for something "urgent." And then suddenly, weeks become months. I've lived that pattern, and I've seen it across teams and organizations. That's why the Monday reset matters.

When I was leading large operations, the environment changed constantly—volume shifts, people issues, customer escalations, new initiatives, and deadlines stacked on top of each other. If I started the week by reacting, I stayed reactive. But when I started the week by stepping back—just long enough to reset focus—I could lead the week instead of being consumed by it. Sometimes that reset took 10 minutes. Sometimes it took 30. But it always saved hours of noise later.

Because leadership doesn't drift when it is reinforced weekly.

The Monday Reset Template (10 Minutes)

Here is a simple structure leaders can use every week. It's not complicated—but it is powerful.

1. **Focus (What matters most?)**

   What are the top 3 priorities this week?

   If everything is urgent, what actually matters most?

2. **Standards (What line cannot move?)**

   What behaviors must stay consistent no matter what?

   What do we enforce even under pressure?

3. **People (Who needs me as a leader?)**

   Who needs coaching this week?

   Who needs clarity?

   Who is carrying too much?

4. **Decisions (What am I avoiding?)**

   What conversation am I delaying?

   What decision do I need to make with imperfect information?

5. **Learning (How am I improving?)**

What did I learn last week?

What do I need to do better this week?

This weekly practice creates momentum. Not because it adds work—but because it prevents drift.

The Leadership Weekly Operating System
How Leaders Prevent Drift and Sustain Execution Discipline

Strong leaders don't wait for quarterly reviews to correct course. They use weekly discipline to reinforce focus, uphold standards, develop people, make decisions, and learn continuously.

From Management to Leadership

Management is about keeping things running. Leadership is about making things better. Weekly discipline is what separates the two.

Without it, leaders default to:

- Solving problems themselves
- Managing tasks instead of people
- Reacting to symptoms instead of addressing causes

With it, leaders shift toward:

- Coaching instead of rescuing
- Setting expectations instead of chasing outcomes
- Building capability instead of dependency

This shift doesn't happen through a training program. It happens through consistent practice.

Why Consistency Beats Intensity

I've seen leaders try to compensate for inconsistency with intensity. They show up strong during crises. They push hard during peak seasons. They inspire when stakes are high.

But leadership isn't measured by how you perform at your best—it's measured by how you behave at your busiest. Weekly discipline creates a baseline. It ensures that values don't disappear under pressure. It keeps standards visible even when results are strong.

Over time, this consistency creates something powerful:

Predictability.

And predictability builds trust.

What This Requires From the Leader

Leadership as a weekly practice requires humility.

It requires admitting that:

- You don't get it right every week
- You will drift if you don't pay attention
- Your title won't do the work for you

It also requires courage.

Because reflecting weekly means confronting avoidance, not just celebrating wins. It means seeing patterns—in your behavior, not just in others'. That level of self-awareness is uncomfortable. But it's also where growth lives.

The Compounding Effect

One strong week doesn't make a leader. But fifty-two intentional weeks do.

Over time, weekly practice compounds:

- Judgment improves
- Decision-making accelerates
- Teams gain clarity
- Leaders emerge around you

Not because of a single breakthrough—but because of disciplined repetition. This is how leaders scale themselves. This is how organizations build culture. This is how transformation becomes sustainable.

Where We Go Next

If Chapter 2 focused on the choice between maintaining and transforming, this chapter focused on the discipline required to sustain that choice. But discipline without ownership doesn't work.

Chapter 4: Leading from the Driver's Seat, because no amount of structure matters if leaders aren't willing to take full responsibility.

Key Takeaways

- Effective leadership is developed through ongoing actions, not just key decisions.
- Regular reflection on priorities and decisions is essential for maintaining focus and momentum.
- Articulating expectations promotes accountability and boosts performance.
- Open communication during weekly reflections strengthens team alignment and trust.
- Commitment to weekly practices encourages your team to adopt similar effective habits.

Reflection Question

What weekly discipline, if practiced consistently, would compound your leadership over the next year?

CHAPTER 4: Leading from the Driver's Seat

Leadership begins the moment you stop waiting. Waiting for clarity. Waiting for permission. Waiting for someone else to fix what isn't working. At some point in every role, leaders face a quiet decision:

Will I observe—or will I own?

I think of this as the difference between sitting in the passenger seat and taking the wheel.

Ownership Precedes Authority

Early in my career, I believed authority came from position. Titles, reporting lines, and organizational charts defined who was responsible for what. Experience taught me something different. Authority may come with a title—but ownership does not.

Ownership is taken.

Leaders who lead from the driver's seat don't wait to be empowered. They don't hide behind ambiguity or defer responsibility upward. They recognize that if something matters—results, culture, people it is their responsibility to act.

This doesn't mean ignoring structure or acting recklessly. It means understanding that leadership is not granted; it's demonstrated.

Drivers and Passengers See the Same Road—But Play Very Different Roles

Passengers and drivers can be in the same car, going to the same destination, experiencing the same conditions. But their responsibilities are completely different.

Passengers can listen to music.

They can watch videos.

They can take a nap.

They can drink coffee and talk about the journey.

Drivers cannot.

Drivers must stay focused. They must watch the road, anticipate risks, make decisions in real time, and adjust when conditions change. They are responsible not just for themselves, but for everyone in the vehicle.

If something goes wrong, no one looks at the passengers.

They look at the driver.

Leadership works the same way. Anyone can be a passenger. Not everyone can—or should—be a driver.

And if you don't want the responsibility of driving, that's a valid choice. But then you don't get to complain about the route.

The Driver vs Passenger Ownership Model

THE PASSENGER

- Waits for direction
- Identifies problems but waits for others to act
- Prioritizes comfort over responsibility
- Mindset: "That's not my role."

THE DRIVER

- Creates clarity and direction
- Owns outcomes
- Accepts full accountability for outcomes
- Mindset: "I'll figure it out."

Leadership begins the moment you stop waiting and take the wheel.

Leadership is not defined by title, but by ownership. The moment you shift from passenger to driver, your leadership impact begins.

Why Passengers Stay Comfortable

Passengers aren't lazy. In many cases, they're capable and well-intentioned.

But passenger thinking comes with invisible limits:

- "That's not my role."

- "Someone else should decide."

- "I don't have the authority."

These statements sound reasonable.

They're also how progress stalls.

Passenger thinking creates distance between leaders and outcomes. When results are good, credit flows elsewhere. When results are bad, blame travels upward or outward. Over time, this mindset erodes credibility—and opportunity.

Taking the Wheel Changes Everything

Leading from the driver's seat requires a different posture. Drivers:

- Take responsibility before they have all the answers
- Make decisions with imperfect information.
- Own outcomes—even when circumstances are difficult
- Focus on solutions instead of explanations

The moment you take the wheel, expectations rise. Visibility increases. Accountability becomes personal.

So does impact.

Responsibility Without Control

One of the hardest lessons for leaders to learn is that ownership does not always come with control. You may be accountable for results without full authority over resources, staffing, or decisions. That tension is real—and unavoidable. The mistake is believing that lack of control excuses lack of ownership.

The strongest leaders I've worked with didn't wait for perfect authority. They built trust, credibility, and momentum by acting as if the outcome mattered to them—because it did.

That mindset is what eventually expands authority.

What Ownership Looks Like in Practice

Leading from the driver's seat doesn't mean doing everything yourself. In fact, the opposite is true.

Ownership shows up in how leaders:

- Set clear expectations
- Make decisions when others hesitate
- Hold standards consistently
- Address problems directly instead of escalating them prematurely
- Develop people rather than rescuing them

Drivers don't remove every obstacle for the team.

They help the team learn how to navigate them.

The Cost of Avoidance

Avoidance feels safe in the short term. It protects relationships. It delays conflict. It keeps things comfortable. But avoidance is expensive.

Unaddressed issues grow. Misalignment spreads. Small problems become cultural ones. Over time, teams learn what leaders tolerate—not what they say they value.

Ownership is uncomfortable. Avoidance is corrosive.

Trust Is Earned Through Ownership

Trust does not flow from authority.

It flows from consistency.

Teams trust leaders who:

- Take responsibility when things go wrong
- Share credit when things go right
- Make decisions aligned with stated priorities
- Follow through—especially when it's difficult

When leaders consistently lead from the driver's seat, trust compounds. And with trust comes influence.

A Posture, Not a Personality Trait

Leading from the driver's seat is not about being aggressive, dominant, or outspoken. Some of the strongest drivers I've known were quiet, thoughtful, and measured. What they shared was not style—but posture.

They saw responsibility as personal. They treated outcomes as shared—but ownership as theirs. That posture can be learned. It can be practiced. And it can be reinforced weekly.

Maintain or Transform Shows Up Here Too

Leading from the driver's seat is a choice.

Maintaining looks like staying comfortable in the passenger seat—waiting, observing, and reacting.

Transforming looks like taking the wheel—accepting responsibility, making decisions, and owning outcomes.

Leadership begins the moment you decide which seat you're in.

Where We Go Next

In Chapter 4, we explored the importance of taking ownership and leading from the driver's seat, emphasizing how true leadership requires accountability and proactive decision-making.

Chapter 5: The Discipline of Focus, we will delve into the critical role that focus plays in effective leadership. Discover how maintaining clarity and prioritizing what truly matters can drive your team's performance and prevent drift in a complex environment.

Key Takeaways

- Leadership starts when you stop waiting for permission and own the outcomes.

- Anticipate risks and focus on solutions instead of adopting a passive mindset.

- Avoidance may seem safe, but strong leaders face obstacles directly and guide their teams.

- Trust is built by taking responsibility, sharing credit, and following through on commitments.

Reflection Question

Where in your current role are you acting like a passenger—and what would change if you chose to take the driver's seat?

Part II — Execution Discipline

CHAPTER 5: The Discipline of Focus

I've walked into meetings where twelve initiatives were labeled "top priority." Twelve. Each had a deadline. Each had an executive sponsor. Each felt urgent.

The team wasn't lazy. They were overwhelmed. Leaders weren't careless. They were reacting. Everyone was moving — but not in the same direction.

When everything is important, nothing truly advances. Confusion doesn't start with bad intentions. It starts when leaders fail to filter. Focus is not a preference. It is a responsibility.

Why Focus Is a Leadership Responsibility

Focus does not emerge on its own. In complex organizations, confusion is the default. Creating focus is not just about saying yes to the right things; it's about having the discipline to say no to the wrong ones.

Curate Your Focus: Leaders must consciously curate their focus, ensuring their teams are aligned with the organization's critical objectives. This requires a proactive approach to identifying what truly drives success.

Clarity Before Action

Speed without clarity creates waste. The most effective leaders pause before acting, asking:

- What truly matters right now?
- What can wait?
- What are we willing to deprioritize?

That pause is not hesitation; it's discipline. It's the ability to step back and ensure that actions align with strategic goals rather than just responding to the latest crisis or request.

Encourage Dialogue: Regular communication and team discussions are essential for maintaining clarity and alignment.

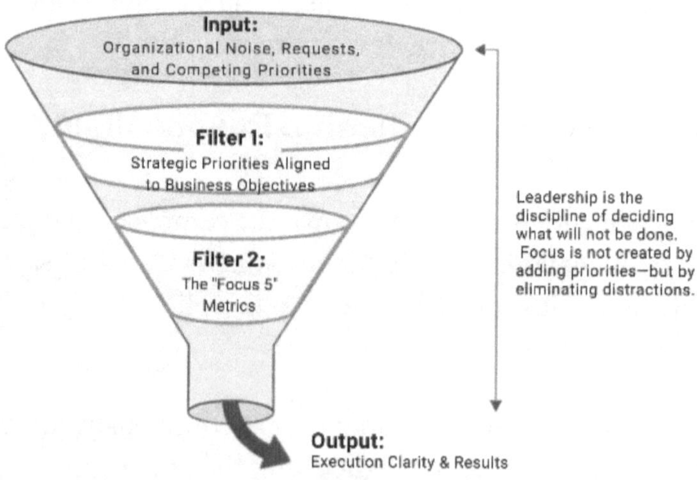

Strong leaders do not accept organizational noise as reality.
They filter aggressively, align strategic priorities,
and translate focus into measurable execution.

A Real Example: Focus at Scale

When I moved into the Senior Vice President role, I noticed not a lack of effort, but a lack of alignment. Operations and warehouse layouts were not standardized, metrics lagged reality, and leaders were held accountable for numbers they didn't fully understand or couldn't influence.

Success was discussed, but rarely defined. Reporting tools were vague and backward-looking, leaving no room for proactive influence. People were working hard but not working together. Instead of adding more initiatives, we simplified.

We standardized processes and layouts, ensuring everyone worked from the same playbook. This created a clear framework for operations, reducing confusion and enhancing efficiency.

We identified a small set of leading indicators—what we called the Focus 5 metrics—that connected daily behaviors to outcomes. We trained leaders not just on the metrics, but on how to change them, redesigning reporting tools to be proactive and visual, allowing teams to see real-time data and understand their impact on performance.

As clarity increased, teams began to understand how their actions drove results. Productivity improved—not from increased expectations, but from enhanced understanding. Leaders transitioned from merely reacting to managing drivers, becoming facilitators of progress.

This shift also fostered a culture of accountability.

Teams took ownership of their metrics, leading to pride in their performance. Over time, this disciplined focus produced double-digit productivity improvements across existing operations and new locations. More importantly, it created sustainable, scalable, year-over-year improvement. This reinforced a lesson I've seen repeatedly: Focus doesn't restrict performance—it multiplies it.

Reinforcing Focus Takes Repetition

Declaring priorities once is not enough. Leaders sustain alignment by repeating priorities, protecting teams from unnecessary noise, and adjusting when facts change. Regular Check-ins: Involve continuous communication about the importance of the Focus 5 metrics, celebrating successes, and addressing challenges.

Additionally, feedback loops must be established. Gathering input from team members on the effectiveness of prioritization can help refine focus and ensure that everyone remains aligned. This ongoing dialogue fosters an environment where focus is a continuous commitment.

Where We Go Next

In Chapter 5, we examined how focus is not just a preference but a core leadership responsibility. By prioritizing clarity and making disciplined decisions, leaders can drive their teams toward success in a chaotic environment.

Chapter 6: Raising the Talent Bar, we will explore the crucial relationship between leadership standards and team performance.

Key Takeaways

- Focus doesn't happen naturally; leaders create it.
- Clarity before action saves time and energy.
- Standardization and leading indicators drive performance.
- Too many priorities create friction and burnout.
- Focus must be reinforced consistently to last.

Reflection Question

What are the three priorities that truly drive results — and what are you allowing to distract your team?

CHAPTER 6: Raising the Talent Bar

"We just need a body."

I've heard that sentence more times than I can count.

The role has been open too long. The team is stretched. Volume is heavy. Pressure is rising. And someone says it — usually with urgency, sometimes with frustration.

"We just need a body."

That sentence sounds practical. It is expensive.

Because the moment you hire to relieve pressure instead of raise the bar, you are no longer solving a staffing problem — you are creating a culture problem.

Talent decisions are rarely urgent because they are easy. They are urgent because leaders have delayed discipline.

Why Standards Matter More Than Intentions

Most organizations don't fail because they set standards too high; they fail because they quietly lower them. Strong leaders understand that standards protect culture. When standards slip, culture weakens.

The Privilege of Being on the Team

When someone joins your team, you grant them a privilege—not because you are more important, but because the team represents standards, trust, and a mission. If the team is strong, people grow, and results follow. If the team is weak, everyone pays the price.

Compromise Is Expensive

Every compromise in talent has a cost. Teams learn what behavior is acceptable by observing what leaders tolerate. Silence becomes permission.

A Real Example: The "I Just Need a Body" Moment

I've faced situations where an opening has lingered too long, and someone says, "We just need a body." That's a warning sign. What follows is predictable: rushed hiring, rushed onboarding, performance gaps, and the team bearing the cost. You don't pay the price on Day 1; you pay it months later.

Hire Like You're Building the Future

When you have an opening, you possess something valuable: choice. Most leaders inherit teams, but with an opening, you can intentionally raise the bar. Lowering standards "just to fill the seat" is one of the most damaging decisions a leader can make.

A Practical Hiring Standard That Works

If the role matters, I want three final candidates evaluated through multiple perspectives.

A strong approach looks like this:

- Three finalists
- Interviewed three different times
- By three different people

This isn't to slow things down; it's to protect standards.

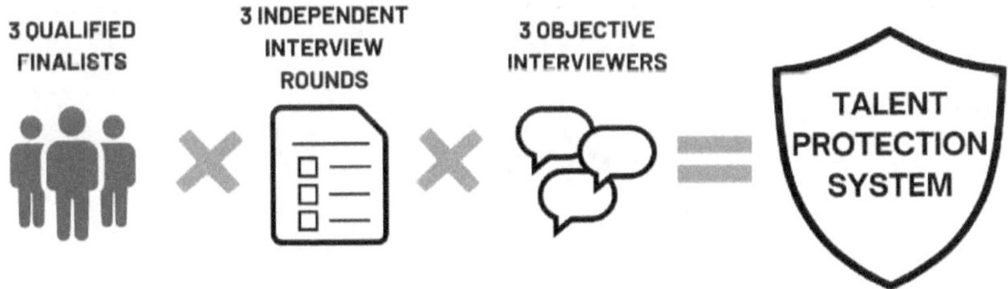

Strong leaders do not delegate hiring standards to chance. They build structured systems that protect talent quality, culture, and long-term organizational capability.

We Inherit Teams—But We Don't Inherit Standards

A leader doesn't choose the team they inherit, but they can choose the standards they uphold.

People deserve clarity:

- What does good look like here?

- What behaviors are expected?
- What will not be tolerated?

High Standards Create Psychological Safety

Teams feel safer when standards are clear and consistently enforced. Clear standards remove tension, allowing people to know where they stand and trust that leadership will act fairly.

Raising the Bar Is Leadership

The best leaders don't use standards to pressure people; they use them to create clarity. They believe people deserve honesty—even when it's uncomfortable.

Where We Go Next

In Chapter 6, we explored the vital importance of maintaining high standards in leadership and how those standards shape organizational culture.

Chapter 7: Lattice vs. Ladder Careers, we will discuss how career development is not solely about promotions but rather about building capability through diverse experiences.

Key Takeaways

- Standards protect culture and performance.
- Lowering the bar "to fill a seat" always has a cost.
- Hiring is a privilege and a responsibility.
- Open roles are opportunities to strengthen the team.
- High standards create clarity and psychological safety.

Reflection Question

Where have you accepted "good enough" in talent decisions—and what would change if you raised the bar?

CHAPTER 7: Lattice vs. Ladder Careers

Most careers are evaluated by title. Strong careers are built by capability. The problem is that titles are visible. Capability is not. Titles are announced. Capability compounds quietly.

For years, career growth was described as a ladder: perform well, move up, repeat. The model feels clean. Linear. Predictable. But leadership rarely develops in straight lines.

The leaders who sustain impact over time do not simply climb. They expand.

The Career Ladder Looks Clean on Paper

The ladder appears orderly, suggesting a clear next step and a visible path. For some, this works—especially in structured industries. However, ladders can create a dangerous belief: if you're not moving up, you're not moving forward. This belief breeds frustration, impatience, and, at times poor decisions. Because careers aren't built solely through promotions, they're built through capability.

The Lattice Is How Leaders Are Really Developed

A lattice career is intentional. It includes lateral moves, resets, and assignments that may not always look like progress. It's shaped by experiences that add range, judgment, and depth—even if they don't add a title right away.

A lattice career might include:

- Moving sideways to learn a new function
- Taking a harder assignment with a higher risk
- Leaving a comfortable role to build capability elsewhere
- Accepting a step back in title to move forward in skill

This is how leaders are developed—not by speed, but by experiences that build strength.

Lattice vs. Ladder Career Development Model

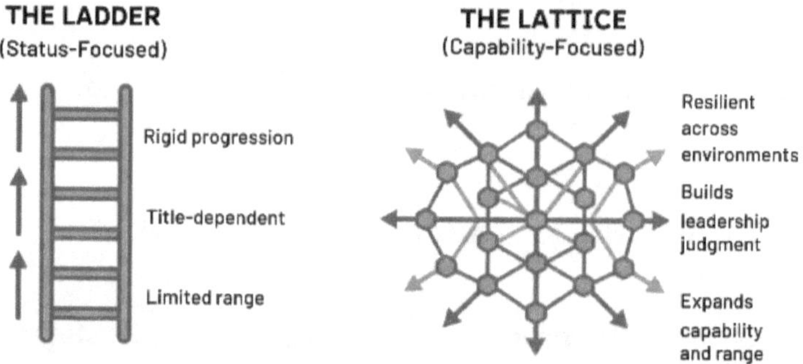

Range builds judgment. Judgment builds credibility.
Credibility expands leadership opportunity.

Strong leaders do not chase titles—they build capability. Over time, capability—not title—determines leadership opportunity.

My Career Was a Lattice Before I Had a Word for It

Looking back, my career was shaped by moves that didn't always resemble traditional success. I moved countries, started over, took roles that required me to prove myself repeatedly, and stepped into environments where the path wasn't clear. I accepted uncertainty as the cost of growth.

Some transitions looked like progress; others, like setbacks. But each added something—resilience, perspective, capability, and leadership range. In the moment, it wasn't always comfortable, but over time, it became an advantage.

Why Lattice Careers Create Stronger Leaders

Ladders reward performance in one environment; lattices build adaptability across environments. Leaders with lattice careers tend to be stronger in three ways:

1. **Learn Faster**: They've repeatedly entered unfamiliar situations.
2. **Build Better Judgment**: They've encountered diverse problems, cultures, and operating models.
3. **Lead with Empathy**: They remember what it feels like to be new, uncomfortable, and underestimated.

The lattice fosters humility, which becomes a leadership advantage.

The Real Metric Is Not Title—It's Range

Range is the ability to lead across complexity.

It allows leaders to:

- Diagnose quickly
- Build trust
- Drive clarity
- Develop people
- Sustain results

Range doesn't come from staying comfortable; it comes from stepping into situations that require growth. That's why I often tell young leaders not to chase the next title too quickly; instead, chase experiences that expand capability.

The Moment You Stop Learning Is the Moment You Start Slowing Down

One of the most dangerous traps in a career is competence without growth. You may become good at your role, deliver results, and feel respected. But slowly, you may stop stretching. The work becomes familiar, predictable, and safe.

That might feel stable, but it can also lead to stagnation. That's when the Maintain or Transform decision arises again. A lattice mindset helps you recognize it early, reminding you that your career should expand, not just advance.

How to Build a Lattice Career Intentionally

A lattice career is not built by accident; it's built by choices.

Here are principles that helped me:

- **Choose roles that build skills, not just status**: If you are learning, you are progressing—even if the title doesn't change.
- **Be willing to reset**: Some leaps forward are preceded by lateral or backward steps.
- **Move toward complexity**: Hard jobs teach what easy ones never will.
- **Earn trust fast**: Every lattice move requires credibility; trust is your fastest path to influence.
- **Stay humble and driven**: A new environment will quickly teach you if you lead with arrogance; humility keeps you learning.

What I Want Young Leaders to Understand

Looking back, I don't see a ladder; I see a series of deliberate choices that built a strong foundation for greater responsibility later.

Leadership is not a race; it's not about the speed of promotion, but the depth of experience. A lattice career may appear less impressive on paper in the short term, but it creates stronger leaders in the long term.

Where We Go Next

If this chapter reframed how careers grow, the next chapter brings it back to the most personal responsibility of all: your development.

Chapter 8: Owning Your Development will explore why the best leaders don't wait to be developed—they build themselves on purpose. This chapter emphasizes the importance of intentional learning and exposure to diverse experiences, ensuring leaders are prepared for future roles and capable of adapting to change.

Key Takeaways

- Careers are built through capability, not just promotions.
- The ladder model creates a dangerous belief about progress.
- Lattice careers foster adaptability and deeper learning.
- Focus on experiences over titles for stronger leadership development.
- A lattice mindset helps recognize growth opportunities early.

Reflection Question

If your career were measured by capability instead of title, what decision would you make differently today?

CHAPTER 8: Owning Your Development

No one will ever care more about your growth than you. And that's not a problem; it's a responsibility.

For a long time, I believed development happened to you: work hard, deliver results, stay patient – and eventually, someone notices. Sometimes that happens, but if you rely on it, you'll wait longer than you should. The best leaders don't wait to be developed; they develop themselves on purpose.

Your Career Will Not Manage Itself

Organizations are busy. Leaders are busy. Business priorities change, and people move on. Even in strong companies with great culture, development can become inconsistent because the system prioritizes results first.

That's why owning your development matters so much. If you don't take responsibility for your growth, you will drift—not because you're incapable, but because no one else has your future on their calendar the way you do.

Development Requires Personal Accountability

Owning your development starts with a mindset shift: you are the CEO of your career. This doesn't mean doing everything alone; it means taking responsibility for what you learn, how you grow, and the opportunities you pursue.

It means shifting from:

- "They haven't trained me yet."
- "No one told me what to do."
- "I didn't get a chance."

To:

- "I'll learn it."
- "I'll ask."
- "I'll figure it out."
- "I'll own it."

Comfort Is the Enemy of Development

Most people don't avoid growth because they're lazy; they avoid it because comfort feels safe. When you're comfortable, you know what works. You've built confidence and routine. But comfort is where learning slows down. The moment you stop stretching is the moment you stop accelerating. The most important development decisions often feel risky rather than progressive.

Development Comes From Exposure

Development is not only training; it's exposure. It involves being placed in situations that require you to adapt, learn quickly, and perform under uncertainty. Challenging assignments are valuable because they teach you what the classroom never will:

- How to lead through ambiguity
- How to influence without authority
- How to build trust quickly
- How to diagnose problems under pressure

That's why lattice careers build strong leaders and why owning your development requires seeking exposure.

A Real Example: Building a Skill Before It Became a Requirement

When I moved to the United States, I recognized a gap—not in work ethic or ability to learn, but in communication. I often felt smarter than I sounded, especially early on when English was my second language. In high-pressure situations, my intelligence and ability seemed judged not by what I knew, but how quickly and clearly I could express it.

At first, that was frustrating. But I realized no one would solve that for me. Instead of waiting for confidence to appear, I treated communication as a skill to build with discipline. I sought opportunities that forced me to improve, putting myself in situations where I had to explain concepts clearly.

Eventually, I created my own training ground. I built and taught a class on financial and warehouse performance for supervisors. It was helpful for them and for me. Teaching forced me to simplify and communicate with clarity, strengthening my confidence, leadership presence, and ability to connect performance to results. This self-development investment paid dividends throughout my career.

Ask for the Work That Stretches You

High-performing leaders often volunteer for hard work—not to suffer, but to gain range. They intentionally choose projects that expand capability:

- Leading a difficult team
- Tackling a broken process
- Working cross-functionally
- Stepping into a new function
- Owning a metric they've never managed before

These assignments create both scar tissue and confidence.

Feedback Is a Gift—Even When It's Hard

Feedback is crucial, especially the honest kind that challenges blind spots and forces growth. Many leaders say they want feedback, but often seek reassurance. Owning your development means having the maturity to seek feedback that helps you improve, even if it stings. It also means being curious, not defensive.

Learn the Skill That Holds You Back

Most people try to improve their strengths, but the strongest leaders focus on their constraints. They identify the skill that, if improved, would unlock their next level. Whether it's technical, leadership presence, or communication, owning your development means confronting your constraints.

Your Development Requires a Weekly Practice

Development doesn't happen in a single event; it happens weekly. Owning your development means creating the discipline to reflect, adjust, and stay intentional.

Each week, ask yourself:

- What did I learn this week?
- Where did I avoid discomfort?
- What do I need to improve next?
- Who am I learning from?

Progress is not accidental; it is built.

Where We Go Next

In the next chapter, we'll discuss something many leaders struggle with for years: being underestimated. Sometimes, the barrier isn't skill; it's perception.

Chapter 9: Becoming an Outsider—and Using It will explore how to turn the outsider experience into an edge and how to lead confidently even when others don't immediately see your value.

Key Takeaways

- You are responsible for your own growth and development.
- Organizations won't manage your career; you must take ownership.
- Development requires personal accountability and a willingness to step out of comfort.
- Exposure to challenging situations is crucial for growth.
- Regular reflection and practice are essential for continuous improvement.

Reflection Question

What capability does your future role require — and what are you doing today to build it?

Part III — Leading Through Complexity

CHAPTER 9: Becoming an Outsider—and Using It

Being an outsider can feel like a disadvantage, but it can become one of your greatest strengths.

For many years, I didn't feel like I belonged, even when I was delivering results and growing. I was still the outsider. At first, I believed the outsider experience was something I had to overcome. Over time, I learned something different: you don't overcome being an outsider; you learn how to use it.

The Outsider Phase Is Real

Early in my career in the United States, I felt like I had to prove myself in ways others didn't. Not because people were intentionally unfair, but because perception is powerful. When English is your second language, communication affects credibility. In some environments, your accent can be mistaken for a lack of intelligence. Your delivery can be judged more than your thinking.

For a long time, I felt underestimated—not for my work ethic or results, but for my communication style in a second language. That outsider experience can break confidence or build resilience.

The Outsider Choice: Maintain or Transform

Being an outsider forces a decision. You can maintain—stay quiet, stay safe, avoid mistakes, and try to blend in. Or you can transform—build skills faster, take ownership earlier, and earn trust through consistency and results. Outsiders don't always have the luxury of comfort, but that pressure can become an advantage. Choosing transformation early builds a lasting leadership foundation.

The Trap: Trying to "Fit In"

Many outsiders fall into the trap of trying to blend in. They stay quiet, avoid making mistakes, and wait for permission. But leadership doesn't reward silence; it rewards ownership. Trying too hard to fit in can hold you back, pulling your focus away from what matters: delivering results, building trust, and developing others. I learned that I couldn't lead from a defensive posture; I had to lead from a confident one.

What Outsiders Learn Faster

Outsiders develop strengths that insiders often don't have to build. They learn how to:

- Observe culture quickly

- Adapt to new environments

- Earn trust faster

- Read a room

- Listen more than they speak

- Build credibility through results

When you don't have automatic belonging, you learn to create it. That becomes a leadership advantage.

Turning the Outsider Experience Into an Edge

I stopped seeing the outsider experience as a weakness; I started seeing it as training. It forced me to build skills I may have delayed otherwise:

- Communication
- Public speaking
- Executive presence
- Structured thinking
- Discipline under pressure

It also forced humility. Humility makes you coachable, and coachability makes you valuable. Leaders who can learn quickly, adapt, and stay grounded become the ones organizations rely on when the environment changes.

A Real Example: When My Background Became the Advantage

At a pivotal point in my career, I realized my background was part of the solution, not a barrier. As a new leader in one of the largest distribution centers during a significant transition, I faced the daunting challenge of implementing changes without fully understanding the history of the facility. I didn't know the stories of many team members or what strategies had been attempted in the past—what worked or what failed.

This lack of familiarity added pressure, as I was tasked with right-sizing the team, redesigning layouts, and implementing new productivity standards. Navigating this complex environment was particularly challenging as an outsider, as I had to prove myself while earning trust from a team that had seen many changes before.

Constant communication became key. By clearly explaining the reasons for change and providing transparent timelines, I fostered trust and engagement among my team

Through this experience, I discovered that my outsider perspective allowed me to approach problems with fresh eyes. By acknowledging my limited knowledge of the facility's history, I created an environment where team members felt comfortable sharing their insights. In the end, the transition was successful, and I learned the outsider advantage: I could lead through complexity by earning trust and fostering collaboration, ultimately turning my perceived disadvantage into a leadership strength.

Outsiders Don't Have to Be Lone Wolves

Strong outsiders build community intentionally:

- Mentors
- Peers
- Sponsors
- Coaches
- Truth-tellers

They find people who challenge, guide, and open doors. Once they gain influence, they do the same for others. One of my leadership shifts was moving from proving myself to developing others.

The Outsider Advantage Is Perspective

Outsiders notice what insiders overlook and challenge assumptions that others take for granted. This perspective becomes valuable at higher levels of leadership because executives get paid for seeing around corners.

What I Want the Reader to Know

If you feel like an outsider—due to your background, speech, appearance, or experiences—I want you to understand this: being an outsider does not disqualify you from leadership; it prepares you for it. Keep building capability, owning outcomes, and developing confidence through results. Your difference can become your advantage.

Where We Go Next

If this chapter highlighted how to leverage the outsider experience as a leadership advantage, the next chapter tackles a prevalent challenge for many leaders: navigating uncertainty.

Chapter 10: Leading Without a Playbook will explore how to make confident decisions in ambiguous situations and drive your team forward.

Key Takeaways

- Feeling like an outsider is real—and it can shape your confidence.

- Outsiders face a choice: maintain comfort or transform through growth.

- Trust is built through transparency, consistency, and fairness.

- Leading experienced teams through change requires clarity, not authority.

- Your difference can become your advantage if you own it.

Reflection Question

How can the perspective that makes you different become your advantage?

CHAPTER 10: Leading Without a Playbook

At higher levels of leadership, the answers don't come in a manual. You're not paid to follow the playbook—you're paid to lead without one.

Early in your career, leadership can feel structured. There are procedures, rules, and examples to follow. But as you grow, the environment changes. The problems become less defined, decisions more complex, and consequences bigger. That's when you realize: there isn't always a playbook.

Ambiguity Is Not the Exception—It's the Job

One of the biggest surprises for many leaders is that senior roles don't come with clarity; they come with ambiguity. You may not have:

- Perfect data
- Complete alignment
- The right people in place
- Time to evaluate every option
- Certainty about outcomes

But you still have to decide. Waiting for full clarity is a form of maintaining. Leadership requires transformation—moving forward with the best information available while staying accountable for the outcome.

The Leader's Job Is to Create Clarity

Even when you don't have all the answers, your team still needs direction. Leaders don't eliminate uncertainty; they reduce confusion by answering questions people are afraid to ask:

- What matters most right now?
- What are we trying to accomplish?
- What will success look like?
- What will change—and what will not?
- What decisions are final, and what is still evolving?

If you can't answer everything, say that. But never leave people guessing.

Communication Is a Strategy

When you lead without a playbook, communication becomes a competitive advantage. Not motivational speeches, but clear, transparent, and repeated communication. Your team doesn't need perfection; they need direction.

Direction requires:

- Frequent updates
- Consistent messaging
- Real context
- Honest timelines

When leaders don't communicate, teams fill the gap with assumptions, leading to rumors and weakened trust.

A Real Example: Building the Model Before You Could Explain It

In one of my executive roles, our business strategy shifted quickly. We were expanding into a new product category with a tight timeline—about six months to build capability, redesign the network, and execute at scale. The complexity created a reality we couldn't ignore: our existing distribution model was not designed for it.

What made it difficult wasn't just the timeline—it was the uncertainty embedded in the transition. The products were not new to the market; they were being distributed by another company and shifting into our network. Historical demand existed, but it was directional rather than precise. Volume assumptions were based on imperfect information, and route density projections were calculated against expected—not proven—absorption rates.

We also didn't know how our go-to-market strategy would influence sales velocity or how quickly the network would adapt to the added variability and new processes. Waiting for perfect clarity would have cost us momentum.

At the same time, the risk was real. If we overbuilt, we would carry unnecessary cost and inventory exposure. If we underbuilt, we would damage service levels and credibility with customers. The wrong sequencing could disrupt existing operations that were already performing well. The decision was not simply operational—it carried financial, reputational, and cultural consequences.

We didn't have a playbook, so we built one. We aligned cross-functional leaders around a single framing question: How do we fulfill this new business without breaking the network?

That question forced disciplined trade-offs. We chose to design a hub-and-spoke model, concentrating a broader assortment in a limited number of regional hubs while protecting velocity and operational stability in spoke locations.

It meant short-term complexity in coordination. It meant building new processes while protecting core execution. It meant asking teams to operate in ambiguity while we refined assumptions in real time.

We built the model before we could fully explain every variable.

In the early weeks, not every assumption held. We adjusted inventory thresholds, recalibrated transportation flows, and tightened communication cadence across operations and commercial teams. The key was not getting every decision perfect—it was committing to direction while staying responsive and disciplined.

The launch ultimately expanded the network's capability without destabilizing performance. But the real lesson was not about the model itself. It was about leadership under incomplete information: define the principles, choose the direction, communicate relentlessly, and adapt without losing standards.

Decision-Making With Imperfect Information

In leadership roles, you will rarely have all the data you want. The question becomes: can you make a decision that is good enough—and make it fast enough? Strong leaders don't confuse speed with recklessness. They make decisions using:

- Principles
- Experience
- Pattern recognition

- Risk assessment

- Input from the right people

Then they commit. Indecision is still a decision, and in most organizations, indecision costs more than the wrong decision.

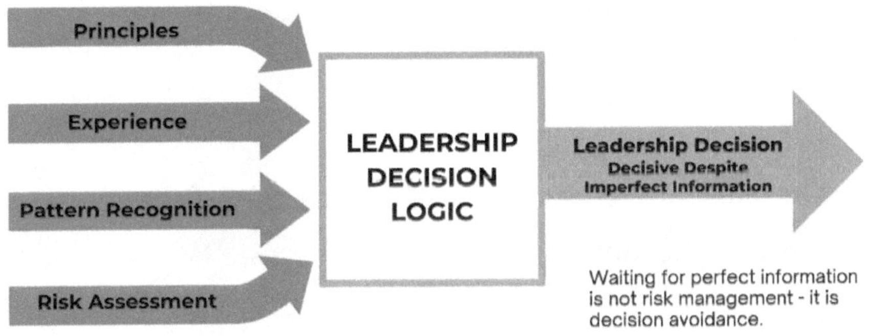

Senior leadership is defined not by perfect decisions, but by decisive action grounded in principles, experience, and judgment—even when uncertainty remains.

Create Alignment Before You Demand Execution

Execution is easy when the organization is aligned, but alignment doesn't happen automatically. When leading without a playbook, the leader must deliberately create alignment by defining:

- Priorities

- Roles

- Responsibilities

- Noise elimination
- Standards reinforcement

People can't execute what they don't understand and won't execute what they don't believe in.

Control the Variables You Can

When things feel unstable, leaders sometimes try to control everything. That's impossible. But leaders can control a few variables:

- Standards
- Communication
- Focus
- Accountability
- Talent decisions

Even in uncertainty, these variables create stability and become the foundation the team can rely on.

Leading Through Pressure Without Losing Yourself

The toughest part of leading without a playbook isn't strategy; it's pressure. Pressure reveals the leader and exposes whether your values are real or only present when things are easy.

The best leaders build discipline before they need it; they don't wait for a crisis to decide who they are.

Where We Go Next

If this chapter focused on the art of decision-making in uncertain times, the next chapter addresses the importance of cultivating trust within your team.

Chapter 11: Leading Change Without Losing People will explore how to guide your team through transitions while maintaining strong relationships and morale, ensuring everyone feels valued.

Key Takeaways

- Senior leadership comes with ambiguity, not certainty.
- Leaders create clarity even when they don't have all the answers.
- Communication is a strategy, especially when information is incomplete.
- Strong decisions come from principles, pattern recognition, and commitment.
- In uncertainty, control standards, focus, and accountability.

Reflection Question

Where are you waiting for certainty instead of leading with judgment?

CHAPTER 11: Leading Change Without Losing People

Change fails when leaders treat people like obstacles. Transformation only works when people feel respected, informed, and supported.

Most leaders understand that change is necessary. Markets shift, customers evolve, strategy changes, and technology moves faster than comfort. The real challenge isn't deciding to change; it's executing change without losing your people. Because results can improve while morale collapses, processes can evolve while trust disappears, and productivity can increase while culture breaks down. That kind of progress doesn't last.

People Don't Resist Change—They Resist Confusion

I've heard leaders say, "People hate change." I don't believe that's true. People don't resist change; they resist uncertainty, lack of clarity, and silence. When people don't know what's happening, they fill the gap with assumptions, leading to fear and engagement drop. Your job as a leader is not to eliminate uncertainty but to eliminate confusion.

Start With the "Why"

If you want people to follow you through change, they need context—not a slogan, but a reason. Change without purpose feels like chaos; change with purpose feels like leadership.

Before rolling out actions, explain:

- Why the change is happening
- What problem it solves
- What staying the same would cost
- What success will look like

People don't need perfect answers; they need clear direction.

Transparency Builds Trust Faster Than Certainty

Leaders sometimes avoid communication because they don't have every answer. That silence is expensive. You can lead through uncertainty if you lead with transparency.

Even when you don't know everything, you can still communicate:

- What you know
- What you don't yet know
- When you will know more
- How decisions will be made

When teams see transparency, they don't feel manipulated; they feel respected.

Change Requires Both Standards and Empathy

Leading change isn't being soft; it's being complete. Strong leaders hold high standards while acknowledging reality. They combine:

- Accountability with patience
- Urgency with clarity

- Toughness with respect

You can push for performance while still protecting dignity. The best leaders do both.

Don't Just Announce Change—Design It

One of the biggest mistakes leaders make is treating change like a message. Change is not a message; it's a system. Change requires design:

- Clear roles
- Defined milestones
- Agreed metrics
- Training and capability building
- Reinforcement mechanisms

Without design, change becomes noise, and noise leads to burnout.

Quick Wins Create Belief

A team won't believe in change just because you said it's important; they believe in change when they see progress. That's why quick wins matter—not for optics, but for confidence. Quick wins show the team:

- The plan is real
- Leadership is serious
- Progress is possible
- Effort leads to results

Belief is fuel; when belief rises, engagement rises with it.

Change succeeds when leaders sequence clarity, trust, execution, and reinforcement—not when they rely solely on authority.

A Real Example: Automation Without Losing Trust

In one of my executive roles, we implemented an automation solution designed to improve how our teams picked slow-moving items in a large distribution facility.

Before the change, selectors spent significant time traveling long distances to pick small quantities. Productivity was steady but inefficient, and we knew the model would not scale as volume increased. The automation system promised better efficiency—but it also introduced uncertainty.

The operational case was clear. The human reaction was not.

Even when a change is framed as efficiency-driven, people often hear something else: job impact, role changes, loss of familiarity. On the floor, questions began to surface—not always publicly. Would this reduce headcount? Would expectations increase? Would performance standards shift? Those concerns are natural, even when the intent is improvement.

The first weeks were not smooth. New processes slowed output temporarily. Supervisors had to adjust workflows. Some high performers resisted because they had mastered the old system and saw no reason to change what already worked. Productivity dipped before it improved.

This is where many change efforts lose momentum.

It would have been easy to push harder and attribute resistance to attitude. Instead, we slowed communication down before speeding execution up.

We reinforced the "why" repeatedly: this was about eliminating wasted movement, reducing physical strain, and preparing the facility for future growth—not replacing people. We clarified what would not change: performance standards, safety expectations, and respect for the team's contribution. We shared early metrics transparently—even when they were not yet impressive.

Over time, the data began to reflect the design. Travel time dropped. Pick accuracy improved. Fatigue decreased. What initially felt disruptive started to feel smarter. Trust didn't increase because we announced change—it increased because we stayed consistent long enough for people to experience the benefit.

Sustainable change is not about speed alone. It is about sequencing clarity, transparency, and execution, so performance improves without damaging culture.

Protect Your Best People During Change

Change increases workload: more projects, more meetings, more pressure. High performers often get overloaded because they are dependable. That is a leadership trap. Your best people will carry you through change, but if you burn them out, you will lose your foundation. Sustainable change requires:

- Balancing workload
- Protecting critical talent
- Clarifying priorities
- Removing low-value work

Leaders don't just drive change; they absorb pressure so the team can execute.

The Maintain or Transform Moment for Leaders

Every change effort creates a leadership test.

Leaders face the same decision we've discussed throughout this book: maintain or transform.

Maintaining looks like:

- Avoiding hard conversations
- Protecting comfort
- Tolerating poor behaviors
- Communicating only when convenient

Transformation looks like:

- Clarity under pressure
- Direct feedback
- Accountability with respect
- Consistent communication

- Protecting culture while raising performance

Change doesn't transform organizations; leaders do.

Where We Go Next

If this chapter emphasized the importance of maintaining strong relationships during transitions, the next chapter will explore the courage required to uphold standards in challenging times.

Chapter 12: The Courage to Hold the Line will focus on how leaders can enforce accountability while protecting their team's culture.

Key Takeaways

- People don't resist change—they resist confusion and silence.
- Start with the "why" before you demand execution.
- Transparency builds trust faster than certainty.
- Quick wins create belief, but communication sustains it.
- Protect your best people so change is sustainable.

Reflection Question

What change are you leading — and where is silence creating unnecessary uncertainty?

CHAPTER 12: The Courage to Hold the Line

Culture isn't what you say you value. Culture is what you're willing to enforce—especially under pressure. Every leader wants high standards. Every leader wants a strong culture. But not every leader is willing to do what it takes to protect them.

Because protecting standards comes with a cost. It requires uncomfortable conversations. It requires consistency. It requires decisions that may be unpopular in the short term.

That is why I call it courage.

The courage to hold the line.

Holding the Line Is Not Being Rigid

Holding the line is not about being harsh. It's not about controlling everything. It means you are clear about what matters:

- Safety
- Performance
- Professionalism
- Accountability
- Respect

You can be human and still be firm. You can be empathetic and still enforce expectations. In fact, the best leaders do both.

Why Holding the Line Feels So Hard

Here's the part people don't always admit: Holding the line feels personal. Because the moment you enforce a standard, you are no longer just managing performance—you are influencing culture. And culture reacts.

You can feel it when:

- Someone gets defensive
- Someone pushes back
- Someone says, "That's not fair."
- Someone tries to test your consistency
- Your team watches quietly to see if you mean it.

And as a leader, you feel the pressure from both sides. You want to protect the culture. But you also don't want to lose your people. You want accountability. But you also understand reality—volume, shortages, turnover, fatigue. That's where many leaders break. Not because they don't believe in standards. But because enforcing standards can feel like choosing conflict.

The truth is:

You're going to pay a price either way. If you enforce the standard, you may face discomfort today. If you don't enforce it, you will face bigger damage later.

Pressure Reveals the Standard

Holding the line is easy when results are good. It's harder when the business is under pressure:

- High volume
- Staffing shortages
- Turnover
- Aggressive timelines
- Customer demands

That's when leaders are tempted to let things slide. And that's when culture is decided. Because teams don't learn what leaders expect. They learn what leaders tolerate.

If the line keeps moving, culture moves with it.

Three Ways Leaders Accidentally Lose the Standard

Over the years, I've seen leaders lose the line in predictable ways. Not because they're weak. Because the moment tests their discipline.

1. **The Crisis Exception**

   Leaders say:

   "We'll deal with it later—we're in crisis mode."

   The problem is: "later" rarely comes.

   And the behavior becomes normal.

2. **The High Performer Pass**

   Leaders say:

   "They're too valuable. We can't afford to lose them."

   But when high performers get exceptions, your real high performers stop trusting fairness.

   And your culture becomes political.

3. **The Shortcut Under Pressure**

   Leaders say:

   "Just make it happen."

   Shortcuts feel like execution in the moment.

   But over time, they teach people that standards are optional when things get hard.

   That's not a performance culture.

   That's a survival culture.

Strong leaders do not avoid accountability conversations. They clearly enforce standards, support improvement, and ensure expectations translate into action.

A Real Example: Holding the Line When Attendance Was Running the Operation

When I was a director running a large distribution center, the challenge was obvious from Day 1. The building was massive—over a million square feet—and the workforce was even bigger. We had more than 500 people, including over 120 selectors, moving high volume every day.

The operation ran almost nonstop. Two shifts. Close to 20 hours a day. Seven days a week. Schedules were built around 4x10s, which meant there were a lot of schedule options. Some were great—early mornings and weekdays. Some were harder—nights, weekends, and peak volume days.

On paper, the system made sense. In reality, the operation was being controlled by absenteeism. Absenteeism was running around 12%. Turnover was extremely high. We were short-handed constantly. On heavy volume days, we needed volunteers to work extra shifts just to keep up.

And that created a cycle that was hard to break. People would call in, then pick up extra hours on the days they wanted to work. Over time, employees were essentially building their own schedules based on personal needs—not business needs.

The bigger problem was this:

The attendance policy wasn't being enforced. Not because leaders didn't care, but because everyone felt trapped.

"If we enforce it, we lose people."

"If we lose people, we fall behind."

"If we fall behind, we create more pressure."

So the line kept moving. And once the line moves, culture moves with it.

A Different Approach: Accountability With Choice

I realized we had to fix two things at the same time:

1. We needed to hold people accountable.
2. We needed to create a system that felt fair.

So we designed a points-based system that rewarded the behaviors we wanted:

- Performance
- Reliability (attendance)
- Accuracy
- And other factors that reflected being a strong team member

Every six months, schedules would be selected based on a ranked list. If you were near the top, you had more options. You could choose one of the most desired schedules—weekday shifts, early start times, or schedules that fit your life. If you were near the bottom, you had fewer options.

The message was simple:

Your actions determine your options.

The Hard Part: Enforcing It

The first cycle told us everything. Some people changed immediately. Others assumed the system wasn't real. So we enforced it. We held the line on attendance. We held the line on expectations. And we let go of people who refused to change their behavior.

That decision wasn't mechanical. Some of those individuals were experienced. Some were well-liked. And in a building already short-handed, every separation increased short-term pressure. There were days when enforcing the standard meant operating with tighter staffing than felt comfortable. But the alternative—continuing to tolerate behavior that weakened fairness—would have cost far more.

Holding the line required absorbing short-term operational strain to protect long-term culture. That part was uncomfortable. But it was necessary. Because without enforcement, the system becomes just another poster on the wall. And people don't follow posters. They follow patterns.

What Happened Next

After the first cycle, the culture began to shift. People saw that the program was real. They saw that performance and reliability mattered. They saw that consistency earned better options. And most importantly, they saw they could control their lives again.

Over time, behavior changed because people wanted to maximize their points and earn a better schedule in the next cycle.

The results followed:

- Attendance improved dramatically
- Productivity improved
- Errors decreased
- Costs improved
- Headcount needs decreased because reliability increased
- Turnover improved significantly

The operation got better. But more importantly, the culture did. We went from a facility where attendance controlled the operation to one where standards controlled the culture—and people had a fair system to win.

That is what holding the line looks like.

Framework: How to Hold the Line Without Losing People

Holding the line doesn't mean being cold. It means being clear.

Here's a simple framework I've used over the years:

1. **Name the Standard**

    Don't imply it. Don't hint. Say it.

    "This is the expectation."

    "This is the standard."

2. **Explain the Impact**

    People change faster when they understand what their behavior creates.

    "When this happens, the team carries it."

    "It impacts safety / cost / morale."

3. **Make Accountability Real**

    This is where many leaders hesitate.

    "If this continues, there will be consequences."

    "This is not optional."

4. **Offer Support (Not Rescue)**

   Support is not lowering the standard. Support is helping them meet it.

   "I want you to succeed here."

   "Let's talk about what's getting in your way."

5. **Confirm Next Step and Timeline**

   No ambiguity.

   "Here's what needs to change."

   "Here's by when."

   "We will revisit this."

Words Matter: Tough Conversation Script

Here's simple language leaders can use:

First conversation (early and respectful):

"I want to be clear about the standard and what good looks like here. This is important because it impacts the team. I believe you can meet it, and I want to support you—but it has to change starting now."

Second conversation (pattern identified):

"We already discussed this expectation. The behavior hasn't changed. This is now impacting performance and fairness. If it continues, we will take the next step."

Final conversation (holding the line):

"I've given clarity, support, and time. The standard is still not being met. For the good of the team and the culture, we are moving forward with the consequence."

This is not about emotion. It's about leadership.

Holding the Line Is Respect

Accountability isn't punishment. It's protection. It protects high performers. It protects fairness. It protects the team from chaos. And it sends a clear message: The standard is real. The culture is real. The work matters.

Maintain or Transform Shows Up Again

Holding the line is a leadership decision

Maintaining looks like avoiding discomfort

Transforming looks like reinforcing standards—even when pressure rises

Standards don't collapse overnight

They collapse one exception at a time

Where We Go Next

Holding the line protects culture. But strong culture doesn't survive on accountability alone. It grows through development.

Chapter 13: Developing Leaders, Not Followers will focus on how strong leaders coach, delegate, and build future leaders through trust and challenge.

Key Takeaways

- True culture reflects what you are willing to enforce, especially under pressure.

- Leadership is proven when challenges arise; shifting standards weaken culture.

- Holding the line involves uncomfortable discussions that are crucial for long-term integrity.

- Establish fair systems with clear expectations to drive behavior change and build trust.

- Provide support to help team members meet expectations without lowering the standards.

Reflection Question

Where do you need to stop letting the line move—and reinforce the standard your team deserves?

Part IV — Leadership That Lasts

CHAPTER 13: Developing Leaders, Not Followers

Results can scale. Systems can scale. Processes can scale. But leadership only scales when you build more of it.

There is a difference between building a strong team and building strong leaders. Strong teams execute. Strong leaders multiply. And the leaders who leave the deepest impact are not remembered only for what they accomplished — but for who they developed.

If people depend on you for direction, you are leading. If people grow because of you — and eventually no longer depend on you — you are developing leaders. That distinction changes everything.

Leadership Development Is the Highest Form of Scaling

As responsibilities grow, one reality becomes unavoidable: you can't do everything yourself. You can work harder, stay later, and take on more, but none of that scales. Leadership scales through people. Your ability to develop others becomes your ability to grow the organization.

The Shift From "Doer" to "Developer"

Early in your career, success comes from execution—you deliver, solve problems, and prove you can handle more. But at higher levels, leadership changes. Your value shifts from what you do personally to what your team can do consistently. That shift requires a new mindset: your job is not to be the smartest person in the room; it's to build the strongest team.

Delegation Is Not Dumping

Many leaders think they delegate, but what they really do is dump work. Real delegation includes:

- Clear expectations
- Context and purpose
- Authority to act
- Support when needed
- Accountability for results

When delegation is done correctly, it develops capability. When it's done poorly, it creates confusion and frustration.

Give People Ownership Before They Feel Ready

One of the fastest ways to develop leaders is to give them ownership slightly before they are comfortable. Not recklessly, but intentionally. Growth comes from stretch assignments:

- Leading a meeting
- Owning a metric

- Driving a project
- Managing a conflict
- Training others

These moments build confidence through action, not theory.

Coach the Person, Not Just the Task

Most leaders focus on execution:

"What needs to get done?"

Strong leaders focus on development:

"Who is this person becoming while doing it?"

That means coaching on:

- Decision-making
- Communication
- Priorities
- Confidence
- Accountability

When leaders coach people—not just tasks—they build capability that lasts beyond a single project.

Feedback Builds Leaders Faster Than Praise

Praise is important, but feedback builds leaders. Not feedback that attacks, but feedback that teaches.

The best feedback is:

- Clear
- Specific
- Timely
- Fair
- Tied to growth

Avoiding feedback doesn't protect people; it limits them.

Leadership is not measured by what you accomplish alone, but by what continues to succeed through the leaders you develop.

The Standard: Build Leaders Who Can Replace You

This is the true test of leadership: if you leave tomorrow, does your team sustain performance? If the answer is no, you may have built reliance; if yes, you built leaders. Developing leaders means:

- Trusting people with real responsibility
- Holding them accountable
- Teaching them how to think, not what to think
- Allowing them to learn through controlled failure
- Celebrating growth, not just output

That's how organizations get stronger.

Maintain or Transform Shows Up Here Too

When it comes to development, leaders face a choice: maintain or transform.

Maintaining looks like:

- Holding the knowledge
- Staying the hero
- Solving every problem yourself
- Keeping control

Transforming looks like:

- Teaching
- Delegating
- Coaching
- Building capability in others
- Creating leaders who can run without you

Developing leaders is not the easy path, but it's the right one.

Where We Go Next

If this chapter highlighted the importance of developing leaders within your organization, the next chapter will delve into the critical role of trust in effective leadership.

Chapter 14: Trust Is the Currency will examine how trust influences execution and team dynamics.

Key Takeaways

- Leadership success is measured by what your team can do without you.
- Delegation is development when it includes clarity and accountability.
- Stretch ownership builds leaders faster than comfort.
- Feedback is a growth tool, not a punishment tool.
- Great leaders build replacements, not followers.

Reflection Question

Who are you intentionally developing — and who is developing because of you?

CHAPTER 14: Trust Is the Currency

You can have the right strategy and the right talent, but without trust, execution will always be fragile.

Trust is one of those leadership topics everyone talks about, but very few people define clearly. Some leaders think trust is about being liked; others believe it's something you earn once and keep forever. Neither is true.

Trust is more practical than that. It's a form of currency that determines how fast you can move, how much resistance you face, and how much support you get when pressure rises. It's also about how much truth people are willing to bring you. In leadership, trust is not a nice-to-have; it's the foundation of execution.

Trust Accelerates Everything

When trust is strong, execution moves faster. Decisions don't get stuck in unnecessary debate. Communication becomes cleaner. Teams take ownership instead of waiting for permission. Conflict stays productive. People assume positive intent and focus on solving problems instead of protecting themselves.

When trust is weak, everything feels heavier—simple initiatives slow down, and progress requires more energy than it should. Most of the time, people aren't resisting the work; they're resisting the leader.

Trust Is Built in Small Moments

Trust is rarely built through big speeches; it's built through consistency. It's built when you do what you said you would do, show up prepared, admit what you don't know, give credit fairly, and treat people with respect—especially under stress.

Trust is earned in a thousand small moments, and it can be damaged in one careless one.

Competence Builds Trust. Character Protects It.

Trust has two sides: competence and character.

Competence asks, can you deliver? Can you execute? Can you solve problems and drive results?

Character asks, are you fair? Are you honest? Are you consistent? Do you do the right thing, even when it costs you?

Leaders need both. Competence gets attention; character keeps loyalty. One without the other creates instability.

The Fastest Way to Lose Trust

Trust is not lost through one mistake; it's lost through patterns.

The fastest trust-killers I've seen are:

- Inconsistency
- Hidden agendas
- Favoritism
- Lack of follow-through
- Avoiding hard conversations
- Blaming others when things go wrong
- Taking credit instead of sharing it

People can handle tough leadership, but they can't handle unpredictable leadership.

Trust Requires Truth

Trust is not comfort; it's honesty.

One of the strongest indicators of trust is whether people tell you the truth—especially when it's not what you want to hear. If your team avoids hard conversations with you, trust is already weak.

Strong leaders create environments where truth is safe. They don't punish feedback, embarrass people publicly, or shut down disagreement.

When leaders respond well to truth, they get more of it, and when truth becomes normal, performance improves faster.

Trust Is Tested During Change

Trust matters most when things are uncomfortable. During change, people are not just watching the plan; they're watching the leader.

They ask themselves:

- Do I believe this leader knows what they're doing?
- Do I believe they care about people?
- Do I believe they will be fair?
- Do I believe they will communicate honestly?

Leaders who build trust early can lead change faster later because they have credibility in the bank.

Trust Is Operational (Not Soft)

In Chapter 10, I shared an example of redesigning a distribution model under a tight timeline. That kind of work only succeeds when trust exists—trust in leadership, trust in the plan, and trust across functions.

When teams don't trust the direction, they slow down, second-guess, and wait for certainty. But when trust is strong, people stay aligned even in the face of uncertainty. They focus on what they can control and solve problems faster. That's why trust isn't soft; it's operational.

Maintain or Transform Shows Up Here Too

Trust is also a Maintain or Transform decision. Maintaining looks like protecting the image over the truth, avoiding conflict, and saying what people want to hear. Transforming looks like being direct and consistent, making fair decisions, and communicating clearly.

Trust doesn't come from intention; it comes from behavior.

Where We Go Next

If this chapter emphasized the critical role of trust in effective leadership, the next chapter will focus on the importance of your leadership brand.

Chapter 15: Your Leadership Brand will explore how your actions and consistency shape your reputation as a leader. We'll discuss the impact of authenticity and self-awareness on your brand, and how these elements influence team perceptions.

Key Takeaways

- Trust accelerates execution; lack of trust creates friction.
- Trust is built in small moments, not big speeches.
- Competence builds trust; character protects it.
- Trust is destroyed through patterns, not single mistakes.
- Trust grows when leaders make truth safe.

Reflection Question

Where does your behavior need to align more closely with the trust you expect from others?

CHAPTER 15: Your Leadership Brand

You don't get to choose if you have a leadership brand; you only get to choose if you build it intentionally.

Most leaders think of "brand" as something for companies—marketing, logos, reputation.

But leadership has a brand too, and whether you like it or not, you already have one.

Your leadership brand is what people say about you when you're not in the room. It's what people expect from you before you speak. It's the reputation you earn through repeated behavior over time.

Your Brand Is Built Through Repetition

Your leadership brand is not built in your best moments; it's built in your consistent moments.

It forms through patterns—how you respond under pressure, communicate when things go wrong, treat people who can't do anything for you, and handle conflict when the stakes are high.

People don't remember every meeting; they remember how you made them feel—repeatedly.

A Strong Brand Creates Trust Before You Arrive

A strong leadership brand creates momentum before you even say a word. When your brand is strong, people assume you will be fair, consistent, and trustworthy.

Your presence creates clarity, not confusion. That is what leadership should feel like.

The Gap Between Intent and Impact

Most leaders have good intentions, but your brand is not built on intent; it's built on impact. This is where many leaders get surprised.

They say, "I didn't mean it that way."

People don't experience your intent; they experience your behavior. That's why self-awareness is not optional; it's a leadership requirement.

Authenticity Is a Branding Decision

Being authentic means being the same person all the time—in good times and challenging times, with the CEO and with the janitor.

People want to know what version of you they're going to get. They can tell when a leader changes depending on the situation, audience, or pressure level.

Inconsistency damages trust, but when you show up consistently—calm, respectful, honest, and clear—people know where you stand, and that becomes part of your brand.

Your Brand Shows Up Most When You're Under Stress

Anyone can look like a strong leader when conditions are easy, but leadership isn't measured in comfort; it's measured under pressure. Your brand is shaped by what you do when plans change, numbers miss, operations are short-handed, timelines are unrealistic, or mistakes occur. Pressure reveals your defaults, and your defaults become your brand.

The Brands Leaders Create Without Meaning To

If you don't shape your brand intentionally, you will still create one. I've seen leaders become known as "smart but unpredictable," "strong but hard to approach," or "results-driven but exhausting to work for." Others earn a reputation for being kind but avoiding hard conversations when accountability is required. None of these are fatal, but they become limiting because your brand will either expand your influence or cap it.

The Leadership Trust and Brand Model

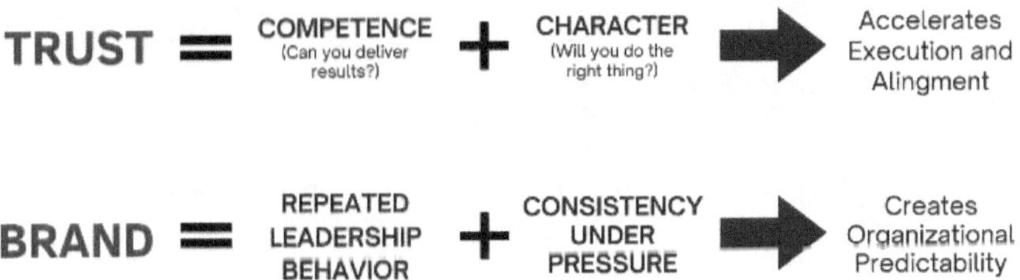

Trust is not a soft skill - it is the currency of leadership execution.

Trust gives you influence today. Brand determines whether you keep it tomorrow.

The Brand That Scales

The strongest leadership brands scale across roles, teams, and organizations.

They are rooted in the same fundamentals: clarity, consistency, fairness, accountability, calm under pressure, and an ability to develop others while still delivering results. People know who you are—not because you tell them, but because you show them.

Authenticity doesn't mean you have to be perfect; it means your values don't change depending on who is watching.

Maintain or Transform Applies Here Too

Your leadership brand is shaped by choices.

Maintaining looks like letting habits run on autopilot, avoiding feedback, and managing perception instead of changing behavior.

Transforming looks like defining how you want to be known and aligning your actions with that standard.

You don't transform your brand with one speech; you transform it through repeated behavior.

Where We Go Next

As we examine the power of your leadership brand, we've discussed how your actions, consistency, and authenticity shape your reputation as a leader. Your brand influences how your team perceives you and affects their engagement and trust.

Chapter 16: Legacy: The Leaders You Leave Behind will explore how your daily actions and decisions shape the legacy you leave. We'll discuss the importance of developing others, fostering a strong culture, and ensuring that your influence endures beyond your tenure.

Key Takeaways

- You already have a leadership brand, whether you built it intentionally or not.
- Your brand is shaped by repeated behaviors, not just isolated moments of excellence.
- How you react under pressure defines your reputation and reinforces your brand.
- Your brand is determined by the impact you have, not just your good intentions.
- Being authentic means showing up the same way for everyone, regardless of the situation.

Reflection Question

If your team described your leadership in one sentence, what would they say — and would you be proud of it?

CHAPTER 16: Legacy: The Leaders You Leave Behind

Your title ends; your impact shouldn't.

When people talk about legacy, they usually discuss big things: awards, recognition, promotions, and numbers. But that's not the legacy that matters most. Sooner or later, every leader moves on. You change roles, change companies, or retire. What remains is not the title you carried; it's the people you shaped.

Legacy is not what you achieve; it's what you leave behind.

Legacy Is Built Daily, Not at the End

Most leaders think about legacy too late.

They wait until the final chapter of their career to ask,

"What did I leave?"

But legacy is built long before that—in daily decisions:

- How you treat people
- What you tolerate
- What you develop
- What you protect

- What you teach through your actions

Every day, you are leaving something behind. The question is whether it's strong or damaging.

Results Matter. But People Are the Multipliers.

I've spent my career in operations and supply chain. I love results and believe in metrics and execution, but here's what I've learned: numbers matter, but people create numbers.

A strong leader can drive performance, but a strong culture drives performance even when the leader is gone. That's the difference between short-term success and legacy impact.

The Greatest Leaders Create Other Leaders

Legacy does not come from being the hero; it comes from building heroes around you.

It comes from developing leaders who:

- Raise standards when you're not in the room
- Hold the line when pressure rises
- Coach their teams the way you coached them
- Create clarity when ambiguity shows up
- Protect culture because they believe in it

That's how organizations get stronger over time—not through one leader, but through generations of leaders.

Legacy Is What You Teach People to Believe

Every leader teaches their team something—whether they mean to or not. You teach people what to believe about:

- Accountability
- Fairness
- Ownership
- Trust
- Effort
- Growth
- What "good" looks like

Sometimes the biggest legacy a leader leaves isn't operational; it's mental.

It's the mindset people carry forward.

You Leave Behind Either Confidence or Fear

I've seen both kinds of leaders.

Some leave behind confidence; people feel stronger after working for them and believe they can do more. Other leaders leave behind fear; people hesitate, avoid risk, and second-guess themselves.

Legacy is not neutral; it always goes in one direction: confidence or fear, growth or hesitation, strength or dependency.

The Leadership Legacy Model

Legacy is not what you achieve; it's what continues because of you.

Leadership legacy is built through decisions, reinforced through culture, multiplied through people, and sustained through the organization you leave behind.

Maintain or Transform Shows Up Here Too

When you look at legacy, it comes back to the theme of this book: maintain or transform.

Maintaining is doing enough to keep the system running. Transforming is building something that improves even after you leave. It's raising leaders, standards, and belief.

Legacy is not built through comfort; it's built through intentional leadership.

The Responsibility of Legacy

Legacy is not accidental. It is constructed. It is built through standards you refuse to lower, through accountability you choose to uphold, and through the leaders you deliberately develop—even when it would be easier to carry the weight yourself.

Your title will end. Your role will change. Your name may fade from the org chart. But the way you shaped people—the confidence you built in them, the discipline you modeled, the expectations you normalized—will remain long after you are gone.

The strongest leaders understand this early. They do not build dependence; they build capability. They do not chase recognition; they create resilience. They do not measure success by control; they measure it by continuity.

Legacy is not built in the final season. It is built daily. Every standard you raise becomes tomorrow's culture. Every leader you coach becomes tomorrow's multiplier. Every system you strengthen becomes tomorrow's foundation.

You may not see the full return on what you build. That is the nature of legacy. Its greatest impact often unfolds beyond your tenure. But that is also its power. Because leadership, at its highest level, is not about what you accomplish while you are present. It is about what continues to grow when you are not.

Final Reflection

If you were to leave your role tomorrow:

- Would your team be stronger because of your leadership?
- Would the culture remain intact due to your efforts?
- Would others be inspired to lead more effectively because of your influence?

This is your legacy, and it begins today.

Key Takeaways

- Legacy is not what you achieve; it's what you leave behind.
- Leaders are temporary; culture and people development are the real impact.
- The greatest leaders create other leaders, not dependence.
- You leave behind confidence or fear—growth or hesitation.
- Transforming means building something that improves after you're gone.

Final Question

If you stepped away tomorrow, what leadership capability would remain because you built it?

You will be measured by the leaders you build—and the leaders they build after you.

ABOUT THE AUTHOR

Carlos E. Gutierrez Ferrete is a global operations and supply chain executive with more than 25 years of experience leading complex, multi-site distribution and logistics networks. Over the course of his career, he has held senior leadership roles responsible for large-scale operational performance, transformation initiatives, and enterprise-level execution.

Originally from Mexico, Carlos permanently relocated to the United States in 2001, rebuilding his professional trajectory in a new market while navigating cultural and operational complexities. He became a U.S. citizen in 2015. That transition—both personal and professional—shaped his disciplined approach to growth, resilience, and long-term capability building.

Carlos has led multimillion-dollar automation programs, network optimization strategies, and large organizational transitions designed to improve efficiency, strengthen resilience, and elevate performance standards. His leadership during periods of disruption—including crisis response and structural reorganization—has focused on building systems and leaders that endure beyond individual tenure.

He is recognized for combining operational rigor with leadership development, building cultures where accountability, capability, and continuous improvement are sustained.

Carlos holds a Master of Engineering in Supply Chain Management from the Massachusetts Institute of Technology (MIT) and a Bachelor of Science in Industrial and Systems Engineering from Tecnológico de Monterrey (ITESM) in Mexico.

He writes and speaks about leadership as a disciplined practice—one built through intentional decisions, structured execution, and the leaders we leave behind.

CONNECT WITH CARLOS

If the ideas in this book resonate with the leadership challenges you are navigating—whether in operational transformation, organizational scale, or leadership development—I welcome the opportunity to connect.

Carlos is open to discussions related to executive leadership, enterprise operations, board engagement, and strategic transformation initiatives.

You may reach him at:

Email: cgutierrez@alum.mit.edu

LinkedIn: https://www.linkedin.com/in/carlos-gutierrez-3982a82/